"He that believeth on me,
the works that I do
he shall do also;
and greater works than these
shall he do because
... if ye shall ask anything
in my name,
I will do it.
— John 14:12, 14

The MIRACLE POWER

by

ROSE DAWN

THE MAYAN PRESS • SAN ANTONIO, TEXAS

10-89

Printed in the United States of America

To
the finest people on earth,
my Beloved Companions
of The Mayan Order

Foreword

DO NOT READ THIS BOOK . . . UNLESS YOU ARE PREPARED TO READ **STRANGE** AND **WONDROUS TRUTHS**

By this warning the mentally-unprepared may, if they choose, avoid being startled by this new Light on old Truths. But the mentally-developed will delight in them.

If you have puzzled long over certain scripture passages, you may in these pages find Enlightenment. You will no longer need to struggle to accept,—or reject, because here if you seek, you will find Understanding; that Rarest Gem, which Solomon declared more precious even than Wisdom.

BE PREPARED, if you read even one page, to feel something pulling you irresistibly back to read them all.

BE PREPARED, if you read them all, that thoughts herein will stay in your mind forever, and will forever subtly change many of your present habits of thinking. If you are fond of thinking you will find new delights with each repeated reading. For the words of this book will conjure up ten thousand thoughts of your own to the thinking reader and thus aid your Spiritual Growth.

BE PREPARED, if you are a thinker, to grow mentally. For each bit of thought you give to these words will multiply within your mind, increasing your capacity in exact proportion as you give thought to it.

BE PREPARED, to ever after find new understanding and new enjoyment of your Church, regardless of your Sect or Creed.

BE PREPARED, also, if you practice these teachings and meditations, to find a Freedom from all Worldly Limitations as a New Path opens before your Enlightened Understanding, and an opportunity to be one of us who, through mental and spiritual forces, have become Masters of our own Destinies.

THE MAYANS

Contents

The Miracle Power

PRELUDE

GOD'S WILL

IN THIS NEW ERA when mankind has not yet recovered from two world wars; while once great nations are reduced to satellites and world powers eye each other with distrust; when science presents mankind with the power in the sun, and mankind's use of it may be for still more destruction; when military experts warn us that the next war will be a "push-button" affair in which giant mechanisms will be hurled through the air at the rate of thousands of miles an hour and half the cities of a nation wiped out in the twinkling of an eye, even before a declaration of war; when economists predict ruinous inflation; when food is so plenteous that it must be "controlled" while millions starve; when communists, conservatists and liberals promise Freedom, but weave new strait-jackets for us to wear; when all these things are taking place at once, is it any wonder that millions of the earth's good people are confused and bewildered? The thinking person is forced to recognize that the greatest need exists for a **Power** to enable us to rise above the dust and turmoil of crumbling international adjustments, the grime of greed and the bloody lusts for authority; to rise above the collapsing social systems; above vitiated monetary systems, above the deteriorations and the recessions, the demoralizations and the pollutions of a waning, crumbling, moldering, blighted and cankered civilization, into a realm where life may be lived as our Maker intended that we should live it.

For it is not true, as many good Christian people have been taught to believe, that "God willed it so."

It is not true, that it is His desire that His children should starve in the midst of plenty, or that the sons of men should hurl death and destruction from His grand blue vault of Heaven down on the heads of their brothers.

It is not His will that millions of men shall be sacrificed in still another Armageddon, or that Commissars, Rulers, Presidents or Kings shall plot new wars and new miseries for His children to suffer. It is NOT true!

It IS true that instead, He placed within every one of us a Miracle Power, a Power to overcome lack and disease and misery, a Power to rise above the horrors of a world gone mad, a Power so wonderful that even in the midst of despair it can provide us in all our needs, can provide us with Peace, can provide us with Plenty.

It is a Power that DWELLS WITHIN US, a Power that is ready for **instant USE,** a Power that is ever present and available to those who will but heed and learn to use it. It is not new. It is as old as mankind. Countless great teachers have proclaimed it. Their followers have been many. But very few have understood the simple Truth of the world's greatest teaching, as given to mankind in the words of Christ Jesus, who said:

"I AND THE FATHER ARE ONE"

And He meant just this — YOU AND THE FATHER ARE ONE. Your being is within Him and He is therefore within YOU. And His Power, His Miracle Power is therefore within you, too. By this Power YOU can accomplish Miracles. With this Power you CAN do Wonders. Through this POWER you can enter Paradise right here on EARTH.

Memorize that Paragraph. Read it again and Under-
tand it. BELIEVE IT. Then read on and start USING it.

What is needed to discover this Power?

Only one thing. You need, you MUST have, a Freedom
From Doubt. Or, to state the same thing more affirmatively,
you must have FAITH.

Faith in What?

Faith in God. Faith in His Supremacy. Faith in His
Miracle Power, indwelling WITHIN YOU.

For that is where God resides. He is not some ancient
Person, existing vaguely somewhere, far off in the skies.
He is within YOU, and through YOU—and all about YOU—
EVERYWHERE. He is through all the Universe because He
IS the universe, the Everything; the ALL IN ALL. And YOU,
beloved, are a part of the ALL; therefore YOU are a part
of Him.

His powers are Your Powers to call upon. In this way
are we ALL made "in His Image." Nowhere in the ancient
writings, of the Bible or other Holy Books, is it taught that
we **look** like God. That is a modern misconception. But in
all of the ancient books it is taught that we are His children,
His creation, and that His love is showered upon us. Meditate
upon this, that Ye may possess the Light of Understanding.

GOD HATH SPOKEN ONCE,
    TWICE HAVE I HEARD THIS,
THAT **POWER** BELONGETH UNTO GOD.
    ALSO UNTO THEE, O LORD,
BELONGETH MERCY:
    FOR THOU RENDEREST TO EVERY MAN
ACCORDING TO HIS WORK.

                        Psalms 62:11,12

Chapter I

The Shape of Things

If you would see the directions and the course in which a river flows, look down upon its valley from a mountain top. If you would see the directions and the course in which flows the stream of life, look down upon life's smoking valley from the viewpoint of the mystics and the gods. A glance reveals twenty-five or a hundred years of history, and the directions in which recent history is pushing us and the slope of the plane. If you dwell in the valley while history is being made, you are too concerned with the details and the worries of every day to gain a panoramic viewpoint. Come up to my Mt. Sinai where the Commandments were written, where prophecies are made, up where the Light first touches and where truth is revealed; where we may discern the shape of things.

—The Author

THE SECOND STORM passed. Some five and twenty years before had been the first one, the Great World War One. Like a mighty whirlwind it had struck, and in insane hurricane force had smashed thousands of homes twisted millions of lives,—and passed on.

Nothing much that was good resulted. The enemy was defeated but the evil was not stamped out. On the Russian front an army wormy with saboteurs collapsed before the Germans and out of the corpse of Russia crawled Communism. That was "the war to end wars." Naive America rejoiced, believing it had turned the tide to win the war. She smiled, her young men, the flower of our nation, had not been sacrificed in vain.

The smile soon faded though as America, unbelieving at first, finally heard her recent allies, Britain and France, and all of Europe calling us "Shylock." We were called worse than that, until red of face and sick at heart, America vowed to have nothing more to do with Europe's eternal wars. Still naive, we imagined we had grown too wise for war to involve us ever again. For a decade we towed our noble battle-wagons out to sea and bombed them down to Davy Jones' locker.

Then came an era of hard times. We called it "the Depression" for we are very fond of new names for old phenomena. No one knew for sure, nor knows today what caused the "Depression" to be so deep, but someone had to be blamed, so blame was laid on President Hoover. Perhaps the Communist Internationalle had a hand in it, for by then Russia had boldly proclaimed she was out to revolutionize the world and in the downfall of Capital that task would be made easier. In any case Hoover was swept out and the New Deal swept in, and the Depression grew deeper and deeper,—and lengthened out. A whole generation of young Americans grew up knowing nothing of better times.

Then came the second storm. It centered at first around a madman called Hitler. With low rumblings the war drums vibrated again. Soon the rumbling became the roar of countless planes, the splitting crash of explosives, the shriek of the wild war-winds mixed with the shrieks and moanings of flesh and blood. Mussolini told with glee of the silly Ethiopians trying to run faster than his planes,—as though they could escape. The horrible Valkyrie swept over Czecho-lovakia and the little democratic nation America had created in Europe was no more. The Russian Bear joined the Hitler Huns and together they destroyed brave little Poland. This was the beginning of the second storm,---but already man forgets.

Britain came into the storm center, and was pushed back, France fell, Belgium, Holland, Austria, Greece, Denmark, Norway, Finland. Then the bad mannered Bear became too much even for the Nazis to stomach and the Bear and the Buzz-saw Swastika went to war with each other. Naive America went to the aid of the Bear as well as the wounded British Lion, but America's leaders who knew where they were taking us never hinted to America what would be the consequences.

What happened had been foretold. In 1908 a hunchback, a seer, and a great military strategist,—an American unsung to this hour, Homer Lee, had written a book in which he told America what would happen. He named the nation, and told what Japan would do, and how, and when. He told of Pearl Harbor, the Philippines and Bataan, he even published maps showing the very route the Japs would take, their complete strategy,—in 1908, thirty-three years before it happened. Yet in Washington they had the audacity to call it "unexpected," to blame it on "the people," and our newspapers to immortalize it as a "sneak attack." Do you care to read Homer Lee's book? You will find it in the libraries at West Point and Annapolis.

The second storm struck America in full fury. But again we had the gift of time, again we barely got mobilization completed. Between eleven and thirteen million of the flower of our nation marched off to war again. Again we turned the tide, again we taste sweet victory. Except that America was saved and the Nazi and the Jap defeated, except for that, again nothing much that is good has so far resulted.

We rationed ourselves and fed the world, both friends and enemies,—and does the world love us? If so, we only hear the curses that are called at us. Dear, sweet, good

America, why must you be hurt -for a third storm may be approaching and this one will not break in distant places, but here on the soil of your homeland. Unless you awake, America, and accept your destiny **now**—not twenty years hence as you imagine—unless you do this, America itself will be torn by the whirlwinds of the third storm.

God has blessed your land, He has made your people abundant. And He delivered by revelation into your hands first the power of the atom. He gave you this, knowing that you would not misuse it to enslave the world. Into your hands, and only temporarily, was given the power to make the world one family, to make war impossible. Monopoly of this power soon slipped away. Other nations found the power and you will be the first some among them would wish to destroy for they know that unless you are destroyed their nefarious schemes will fail, and when you are destroyed the rest is comparatively easy. And this is NOT a preachment of war but of Peace.

I will not take your time talking about the thermonuclear bomb. No matter what you have read or have been told about it, the power of the atom is greater than you think. Guided missiles now travel at unbelievable speed, and soon other devices will go faster and farther. Scientific advancements make it possible to launch fleets of such devices carrying nuclear war heads to any spot on earth within minutes, not hours -without the necessity of a single human on board. Radar will make it possible to sit in an office in Washington, San Francisco, Kansas City, anywhere, and see what is taking place in the streets of Cairo, Paris or Bombay. New poisons and gases are known to all the great nations, whose effects are far worse on humanity than D.D.T. is to the insect world. And there are many more devices completed and worked out, in possession of various countries, of which I dare not even speak.

No nation remains long the exclusive possessor of any of these secrets.

The Third Storm is gathering. Its first effects will be economic; probably the destroying fever of inflation, followed possibly by the chills and ague of deflation. The storm will strike, if strike it does, in the midst of the chills and fever. We have this much warning.

Is all this inevitable? No, it can all be avoided. But we are traveling the road, racing down the road that leads to all this. Only the Power of a Miracle can save us.

The original edition of this book, instead of the fore-going prophecy and warning, contained a chapter titled "The Coming Conflagration," which held a veiled prophecy of the (then) coming Second World War. All the rest of the book is exactly as it was originally written in 1938 and published early in 1939. The storm of war has come and gone again since those days. Thousands of copies went to war with our boys and many are the letters telling of miraculous escapes owners of this book experienced. There seems to be something miraculous in the book itself as well as in its words; for it has changed the lives of thousands. Let it work miracles in your life too, for it has proven the be-ginning of miracles.

Rose Dawn.

Chapter II

Building Your Future

"For nation shall rise against nation . . . and there shall
be earthquakes in divers places, and there shall be
famines and troubles: these are the beginnings of travail."
Mark 13:8

WHEN THIS BOOK was first written, in 1938, the chapters
devoted to a warning of the coming inflation seemed
foolish. From 1929 to late 1936, America had seven lean
years, the longest depression in our history. In 1937, Prosperity reappeared suddenly and for a few months things
boomed. Then the economic tinkers passed the "death sen-
tence act" and business withered, sickened and a new depression got under way in 1938. The depression again
became the "normal" way of life.

In the face of this, Mayan prophets warned of a coming
world-wide inflation. The Miracle Power warned America
to have nothing to do with inflation here, regardless of how
seductive its early effects might appear. No nation has yet
been able to control real inflation once it has begun. The
seeming gains of high wages are a mockery. Excess in
ANYTHING is bad.

People disbelieved the prophecies of Rose Dawn on the
radio, that world-wide inflation was ahead. Yet today,
and for several years past, inflation has taken over in

many of the earth's nations. In Greece it has reached the depths, in China it has reached such absurd degree that a single meal in Chungking, Life magazine reports, costs $10,000.00. Italy and France, Mexico and Argentina, and many other nations are far along inflation's path.

Like a narcotic, in its early stages people enjoy inflation. It is a direct result of dishonesty in economics, greed and excess. Once it passes a certain stage there is no stopping it until money has lost all value. All the world is wondering what will come next and the people who saved their earnings are worried about how they will preserve that which they have worked for, if full inflation comes to America.

Roger Babson, the world's most quoted financial adviser, in his book "If Inflation Comes," is able to offer only one investment as a hedge against the days to come. He reviews all possible types of investments, then points out the dangers, the unsubstantiality of them all when inflation comes.

"There is no way to **make** money," he says, "during a period of inflation. The reason is that if you sell to take a profit, there is nothing to buy which has not gone up as much as what you sell!"

In his book Babson goes on to point out that Stocks, Bonds, Real Estate, Railroads, Manufacturing, Shipping, none of these make a safe investment during inflation. The employee and the employer are equally harassed. The man with money soon finds himself no better off than the man without money.

"There is only one REAL hedge against inflation," says Babson, "and that is, an investment in CHARACTER."

"One of the great difficulties today is, that during recent years, voting privileges have increased through Universal suffrage; transportation has increased through automobiles; vision has increased through moving pictures; hearing has been multiplied a thousand times through the radio. Yet in that same period there has been almost no increase in the nation's character;—that is, in our Faith, Self-Control, Judgment and Courage. A sane faith, with a philosophy of life is of great worth irrespective of the value of the dollar."

Babson then points out that in order to possess Character, we must have culture,—not necessarily the culture that comes from an attendance at college, but, as he puts it, "We were created with a brain and with the power to see and hear, as well as with a stomach with the power to eat and sleep,"—and he shows how culture brings pleasure and joy even in simple things and thus it, too, is a hedge against the day that is approaching.

A man cannot be poor if he has friends. For friendships are the realest of riches and neither are they subject to the fluctuating values of inflation. Thus, friendship, says this great man of the financial world, Is a very real hedge against inflation.

"True friends understand us, sympathize with us, and always trust us. Moreover, most of us do not know who our real friends are until we do have troubles."

Then Babson points out a most profound truth. He says, "If a nation should spend one-twentieth for helping other nations and developing friendships with other nations, what it spends on battleships and armament, how much better off the world would be."

And in this statement Babson reveals his own development of Character, Culture and that feeling for humanity that we mean when we speak of Divine Love.

These three, Character, Culture and Love, in our make-up, is what determines the voltage of our Miracle Power. We all possess this Power but with some, it is static, inactive or lethargic. But by stirring up these three, by activating them through contact with their Source, we make the Miracle Power active in our lives and through us affect other lives.

Verily, it is true, if we would give but a fraction to others of the effort expended to beat them or surpass them, the whole world would be bettered, but most particularly would we ourselves be improved. It was stated many years ago in these words:

> "GIVE AND IT SHALL BE GIVEN UNTO YOU; GOOD MEASURE; PRESSED DOWN, SHAKEN TOGETHER, RUNNING OVER."

But permit me to quote the final words of Babson in his remarkable book written for the guidance of the monied men of our country, if inflation comes. He says:

> "A final thought . . . I must say one word about prayer, quietness and worship. Although I am a horrible example and perhaps a hypocrite in the minds of many, I would be much worse were it not for my daily 'quiet hour.' As soon as possible after lunch each day, I take a brief nap, after which I have a quiet twenty minutes in private worship. The busier my day and the greater my responsibilities, the more particular I am to have this quiet period. I try to read a little scripture, a short prayer . . . and then spend a few minutes in Meditation.

"Faith and Power has come to me during these short daily quiet periods. I EARNESTLY RECOMMEND THEM TO EVERY READER.

> "Periods of Meditation are absolutely free, like the air and sunshine, equally to everyone. There are no exceptions to this statement. This is another proof that the most valuable things, the most wonderful things, and the most beautiful things, are not the advertised, commercial and popular things. The 'still small voice' which comes to one in quietness and worship is a thousand times more important."

If Babson were not already known as a great man, as a man unique in the American scene, these words of his would alone testify to his greatness, his perception, his culture and his character. For he proves by these words, if not by his tremendous wealth, that he has found the Key to The Miracle Power,—that he has discovered the door by which to enter the inner world where one may draw Strength and Wisdom direct from the Creator who is in and through the Universe.

Small wonder that he has been able to accurately predict for years every major upward swing or downward swoop of the stock market and to help countless investors to attain wealth;—small wonder,—for he has touched The Miracle Power.

Small wonder that he realizes that money, as money, is worth very little. That the things of real value, of lasting worthwhileness, are the immaterial things that only grow stronger and greater in adversity. Make the most of this wise man's advice.

Develop your CHARACTER, gain in CULTURE, develop FRIENDSHIPS, express DIVINE LOVE.

In the words of Jesus as written in Luke 12:22 to 34:

> "And He said unto His disciples, Therefore I say unto you, be not anxious for your life, what ye shall eat; nor yet for your body what ye shall put on.
>
> "For the life is more than the food, and the body more than the raiment.
>
> "Consider the ravens, that they sow not, neither reap; which have no store chamber nor barn; and God feedeth them: of how much MORE value are ye than the birds.
>
> "And which of you by being anxious can add a cubit unto the measure of his life? . . .
>
> "But if God doth so clothe the grass in the field, which today is, and tomorrow is cast into the oven; how much more shall He clothe you, O ye of little faith?
>
> "And seek not what ye shall eat, and what ye shall drink, neither be ye of doubtful mind. For all these things do the nations of the world seek after; but your Father knoweth that ye have need of these things.

"Seek ye His kingdom, and these things shall be added unto you.

"Fear not little flock; for it is your Father's good pleasure to give you the kingdom.

"Sell what you have, and give alms; make for yourselves purses which wax not old, a treasure in the heavens that faileth not, where no thief draweth near, neither moth destroyeth.

"For where your treasure is, there will your heart be also."

Purses which wax not old,—CHARACTER, CULTURE, FRIENDSHIP, and DIVINE LOVE, . . .

Chapter III

What The Miracle Power Is

LET US START by saying that the Miracle Power is not anything supernatural, in the sense that it transcends or supersedes nature. Instead it is the essence of Natural Power, for it is the Power of God.

"If it is natural, how then, is it miraculous?" you may ask.

It is miraculous only because it is so different from what most of us have experienced, - we have drifted so far away from God,—from the natural, the real and the genuine. We live in a world of machines and clocks, where time is measured out in neat little sharp cornered parcels of seconds, minutes, hours, days and weeks. We exist in such a multiplicity of man-made laws that each day we transgress many of them, and so fear the consequences that we give little thought to God's laws.

We so fear being unable to pay the rent or to buy food that our thoughts are all of snatching and grabbing instead of giving and loving. We scurry and sweat and beat and rob in our competition for Success,—then wonder why it is that we get back from the world we compete against, the same sort of meannesses.

"Self-protection makes this necessary," you say?

No, my friend, you are wrong if you believe that.

Was it really self-protection that caused Hitler to take Czechoslovakia, or caused Mussolini to take Ethiopia, or caused Japan to enter China? I think not. Nor is it self-protection to gain personal advancement by beating down a fellow-worker, or to show him up, or to stand upon a fallen foe and crush him into the mire.

Let me show you instead how reasonable and right the Miracle way works.

Suppose that you were employed in an office. It would be natural that you desired advancement to a better post that paid more money.

Now suppose that there was working with you, another person who might stand in the way of your promotion according to your views. That is, we'll say, he was older in point of service and first in line for the better position. Now suppose that you knew that he was a shirker or that he did not do his work well. You could find several ways to show him up, perhaps even cause him to lose his job, and thus climb over his shoulders to the better position. That is the way most ambitious people TRY to get ahead.

But even if one succeeds in getting ahead in that manner, he has made an enemy. An enemy who will undoubtedly try to get revenge. But whether he succeeds in hurting you or not, you will have lost some of the esteem of your fellow-workers. And even if they never know by what trick you did it, you will have lost something of Character and your own self-esteem, which is the worst loss of all.

Now, suppose instead, you were to apply The Miracle Power of GIVING. Suppose, instead of plotting against your shirking fellow worker, suppose you gave him your help; your assistance and your friendship. Suppose by Your Example, you did everything possible to make him a better worker, a more honest employee. If you succeed, your firm is better able to give you both an increase in salary. If you succeed, your department begins to boom, to attract the attention of the man that gives the raises. And he will soon discover for himself who deserves advancement the most. You have made a friend of the one who would have been an enemy, you have gained the esteem of your fellow-workers, and you have grown in Character and Self-Confidence, and you have helped your firm to greater Success. You have made a worker out of a shirker, and you have gained the promotion which you desired, but best of all, you can apply the same principle again and again for future promotions and advancements.

"GIVE AND YOU SHALL RECEIVE: GOOD MEASURE, PRESSED DOWN, SHAKEN TOGETHER, RUNNING OVER."

That is the teaching to follow to work miracles.

But you must notice that word "Give" comes first. And you **must GIVE** in good measure and pressed down and running over. For accordingly as you Give, will you most surely Receive.

The above is but ONE example of the giving.

But the principle applies to everything in life. EVERYTHING! It is one of God's Miracles. It is TRUE. It is therefore LAW. It does not fail. There are no exceptions to it, if the giving be genuine. Rewards always come from giving. True, the rewards may be somewhat different than we anticipate. Or they may come in some way other than we expect, but come they do,—ALWAYS.

God's first act of creation as recorded in Genesis was to give the Gift of Light. By the Light we are able to see, and thereby to Understand.

By the Light of Understanding, we develop THE MIRA-CLE POWER. And the Miracle Power in turn will Light up your Understanding so that it shines back; reflecting back to its source and giving out to all others—a Guiding Light—a light to illuminate other minds,—and still others,—until by all the galaxy of their shining, heaven itself is duplicated right here on earth.

Can you sense it?—There IS a Guiding Light leading you . . .

Chapter IV

God Is All – All Is God

WHEN I was a child I often used to look up into the sky and imagine I would someday build a ladder up to the beautiful fleecy clouds, there to dwell happily, away from all the beating turbulence of the life about me. And again at night I would gaze up at the moon and stars sailing so serenely in space.

But at night there seemed such a vast emptiness between me and the stars, – so much vacancy. My understanding then was that all this space between was a sort of vacuum. Later, I learned that the seeming emptiness was filled, – with a peculiar substance that scientists called "ether," but it still seemed rather empty and lonely to me.

It was not until I grew up that I learned the saying that "nature abhors a vacuum" and it began to dawn on me that all this vast, limitless, infinite space was filled to the brim with the realest sort of substance. Invisible to human eyes, yet substantial enough to support the weight of the earth and all the countless millions of planets that float on their courses through it. A Universe, – ALL of Creation, filled and brimming with the Spirit of Life, – I came at last to realize that this invisible substance, this Spirit of Life, also penetrated everything.

Science now recognizes part of this Truth, in its efforts to discover how "Cosmic Rays" have the power to change, to metamorphose into visible material substance. But I have learned that everything constantly changes,—that nothing remains as it is, nor quite as it was, but moves as though in a tremendous spiraling circle within itself. The earth has its orbit, but the orbit too has a path that spirals endlessly on through other circles. And the spirit of life crystallizes into some material form, animates it for a time, then leaves it for the greater freedom of unmaterial existence, and all the stars, the planets, the comets, the constellations change, even as do I.

And things that seem unchanging here on earth do change, but at different rates of speed, sometimes too rapid, sometimes too slow for our limited physical range of perception. We can watch the sea waves roll and break on a rocky shore, but we are not aware that very slowly this same motion is occurring on the land surface of the earth. We can see the mountain ranges and they seem unchanging, but it is difficult for us to realize that they are even now slowly rising, breaking and falling, duplicating exactly the actions of the ocean's waves. We hear of earthquakes occurring here and there on the earth's surface, but we do not think of them as being akin to an exploding surf. Their movement is so slow compared to our rate of perception.

A glacier's movement is measurable though scarcely visible to our perceptive range. But how unutterably fast its motion; how furiously brief its life, compared to geological time. And on the other hand, compare the slow beat of time upon the Rocky Mountains and their life span, compared to the brief few hours that encompasses birth, maturity and old-age for the drosiphila or fruit-fly.

Change, Change, Change everywhere, constant, ceaseless, unending change. Nothing in physical life is eternal but change. But all change follows a pattern, the difference being chiefly one of frequency; of vibratory speeds. Over and under and through it all is One Principle of LIFE ETERNAL; but constantly working, churning, growing, changing, evolving. There is no standing still in the Universe.

The snail crawls his course, the man walks his path, the bird flies his span, the earth rolls its orbit and the Universe spirals a circular space. Seconds, minutes, hours, days, weeks, months, years, decades, epochs, eras, ages, eons, cycles, all are in motion. Nothing stands still. Everything moves,—and changes as it goes.

A single bit of protoplasm is used in modern laboratories to demonstrate the eternal qualities of life, even in the physical form. Dr. Alexis Carrel, at Rockefeller Institute, not only kept a piece of chicken heart alive, but growing, in a chemical solution for a period of more than thirty years. It lived by growing and grew by living.

And thus, this insensate bit of flesh living far, far beyond its normal lifetime should teach us all a secret: "Grow, by living, O Proud man;—Live, by growing, for you cannot stand still. You must shrivel and die,—or grow. Expand your interests, grow in mentality, develop your immortal soul, feed your eternal spirit. Grow,—by Living."

In the preface of his book, "Man the Unknown," Dr. Alexis Carrel points out one of the cardinal teachings of our Mayan Order. He says:

". . . . Because men cannot follow modern civilization along its present course, because they are degenerating,—they have been fascinated by the beauty of the sciences of inert matter. They have not understood that their body and consciousness are subjected to natural laws, more obscure than, but as inexorable as, the laws of the sidereal world. Neither have they understood that they **cannot transgress these laws without being punished.** They must, therefore, learn the necessary relations of the cosmic universe, of their fellow men, and **of their inner selves,** and also those of their tissues and their mind."

Speaking of chemical relations of the body, Carrel says: "Man is, first of all, a nutritive process. He consists of **a ceaseless motion** of chemical substances. One can compare him to the flame of a candle, or to the fountains playing in the gardens of Versailles. Those beings, made of burning gases or of water, are both permanent and transitory. Their existence depends on a stream of gas or liquid. Like ourselves, they change according to the **quantity and the quality of the substances which animate them.**

"As a large river coming from the external world and returning to it, matter **perpetually flows** through all the cells of the body. During its passing, it yields to tissues the energy they need, and also the chemicals which build the temporary and fragile structures of our organs and humors. The corporeal substratum of all human activities originates from the inanimate world and, sooner or later, goes back to it. Our organism is made from the same elements as 'lifeless things.'

"Therefore we should not be surprised, as some modern physiologists still are, to find at work within our own self the usual laws of physics and of chemistry as they exist in the cosmic world. Since we are parts of the material universe, the absence of these laws are unthinkable."

Indeed this is true. One Universe and One Creator which is Eternal,—and we are parts of the All. We cannot transgress the Laws of the Universe without being punished. We live and grow Mentally and Spiritually by what we feed upon. We change according to the quantity and the quality of the substances we feed upon. And this is true of you, in each of the departments of your being, of your physical body, of your Mind, your Spirit and your Soul.

Long years ago a wise man said, "Thoughts, are things."

In other words, thought, is the unmaterial substance. The architect, the inventor, the writer, all create first in thought, then build the material substance into the pattern which they first created mentally. You can do this with your life. The same principle applies.

First, visualize what you want to be. Not in an idle, dreamy, wishful sort of way, but dynamically, definitely and with a strong lasting DESIRE. Create the **Vision.** Make it definite,—exactly what you want to be. See yourself **being** it. Then start living the part.

If you hold that vision unchangingly, live that part unwaveringly, you gradually grow that way until you actually **become** what you want to be. It matters little **what** it is. No matter how remote it may seem from your present personality. You CAN become anything you wish to be if you BELIEVE that you can, and live the part constantly. You grow by living, and your growth is a ceaseless changing according to the quantity and the quality of the substances which animate you. And that quantity and quality are determined by the substance of your THINKING.

The greater part of you is invisible. We are all inclined to visualize ourselves according to our physical appearances, thinking consciously only of our physical body. But Mind is greater than body. And so is our Spirit and so is our Soul. Yet these three parts of You, even though greater than the body in importance because they are truly immortal, are all invisible to our present perceptive abilities. How much more important it is to give **them** substance, to animate them that they may live and grow, than merely to feed the physical part.

We know that if we do not feed the physical body at all, it will wither and die. We know that we cannot transgress this law without being punished. How much more essential it is that we also feed the Mental, Spiritual and Soul bodies of our being. For we cannot transgress the Law here either. But if instead, we live in harmony with the Law, transgressing it not, our capacity is increased in proportion to our growth. Our abilities enlarge and multiply. Our joys increase with our appreciations. In this way, and this is the real way, we attain Heaven, no matter where our physical body may be, and even though it may cease to exist as a physical body.

So now we turn to the question of what constitutes food for our invisible bodies, and how such substance may be fed and how its quality may be determined. Which brings us to the first miracle,—the Miracle of The Guiding Light,—that "something" which we perceive at first only dimly and deep within our consciousness and which we usually refer to as our conscience. The voice of conscience is tied up very closely with that Recording Angel which dwells in our Soul and which we call Character.

The Miracle is this,—that in every act and in every thought we think, the Angel records upon our Character, either good or bad, and something glows within us, like a light showing us the right way, while an inner voice speaks, telling us what is right for us to do.

We can close our consciousness to the Light, and we can ignore the Voice if we choose, but we can never blot out the record on our Character and if we transgress we will be punished and if we do right we will be rewarded. Long after active memory has allowed us to forget, the record stands imperishable. The Miracle is in the sure knowledge of what is right and what is wrong, which flashes into our consciousness. We can numb our consciousness to it by repeated transgressing, by refusing to heed it, by ignoring it, but we cannot escape the punishment. Or, we can attune our consciousness to it and eventually avoid all error and not only that, but by ever closer attunement even become prodigies, accomplishing all manner of miracles.

For that inner voice, that Guiding Light, is the part of us that is "in the image of God."

It never fails to distinguish good from evil regardless of how we may attempt to deceive our conscious selves. For most certainly if God is All-Powerful, then He is Universal, Omnipresent, and Omnipotent. And, it follows that if the Creator of All **is** Universal, then we are a small part of Him. He therefore dwells in us. And, necessarily, **we,** therefore, have our being in Him.

If His Power extends in and **through** all the Universe and we are a part of the Universe, it also extends in and through us. We, therefore, possess a small part of His Power. Thus, are we in His image.

At least a small part of His wisdom is in us and by learning to attune our consciousness to it, we can become many times wiser than we are when depending on our conscious wisdom. Not in His "shape," but in His Image.

The door to becoming more perfectly in His Image is our Imagination. For "Creative" Imagination is also a department of our Soul-body. The Path is Faith. The means, is Meditative Prayer.

These three, Creative Imagination, Faith and Meditative Prayer, are the triune transmitters of The Miracle Power.

The Miracle Power comes from God Himself and is given unto all mankind. That we possess it is evidence that we ARE made in His image.

"And God **created** man in his own image, in the image of God created he him; male and female created he them. And God blessed them;"

The above passage is from Genesis 1:27 and refers to the SPIRITUAL Creation of Man in the Image of God. But it is not until later, in Genesis 2:7, that we are told of man's PHYSICAL shaping.

"And Jehovah God **formed** man of the dust of the ground and breathed into his nostrils the breath of life . . ."

Our likeness to our Creator is not in the physical body but in the three higher bodies of Mind, Spirit and Soul which compose our Immortal Being. God is all, and All is God.

Thus have I been taught by The Mayans. Thus do I believe . . .

Chapter V

Miracles For You

UPON ENTERING the lovely little Prayer Room of the Chapel of Miracles maintained by the Mayan Order, one finds at his right side a stained-glass window reaching up to the ceiling, and picturing the ascending Christ. Directly before him is a prayer altar where daily prayer is observed by certain of The Meditators.

A carillon chimes softly at the appointed time of the Angelus Call when members of this Order everywhere from the Atlantic seaboard to far off Hawaii, from the mountains of Central America to Northernmost Alaska, stop whatever they are doing and in unison turn their thoughts in Meditative Prayer for all those who have called upon the Mayan Order for Prayer.

Hushed and shadowy is this room. One's eyes must become accustomed to the light streaming through the window before he becomes aware of the great number of written prayers that repose on the altar of prayer.

And as the Ceremony of the Angelus Call continues, one seems to actually feel the thoughts of faith and hope coming into this holy place from thousands of supplicants.

A mysterious breeze springing seemingly from nowhere rustles the written prayers as though Angel hands were touching them, while the prayer-period progresses.

And to this place an increasing tide of written prayers pour in. Each new day's mail brings joyous messages of relief, of gladness, of success, of Prayers fulfilled, of miracles. With each glad tale of a faith fulfilled, of a miracle, new converts are made and new names of people appear, who wish to try a "written prayer."

The Preceptor in charge explains to me that often when one is deeply troubled and he can see no way open before him, he may become confused and find it difficult to concentrate his thoughts upon a spoken prayer. But the very act of writing necessitates concentration. The act of sending a written prayer to this far away cloistered room stimulates the imagination. The testimony of others who have experienced miraculous results creates an attitude of expectancy so necessary for gaining results. The knowledge of the good works performed and the sincerity of the many minds united in Prayer over all of North America gives faith to the wavering. Small wonder that so many miracles have been reported here.

Medical science has long been divided in its opinions on the healings accomplished through prayer. Yet I have noted that the older physicians and the most famous scientists are usually first to declare that miracles do happen. It is usually the young "know-it-alls" who are not yet convinced.

This does not mean that in Mayanry, science is discounted. On the contrary, in the wonderful Revelations which all members receive, the world's great scientists and their opinions are reviewed and many people are startled to learn that there is no quarrel between science and religion, when the science is deep and the religion real. True, there are surface misunderstandings on both sides, but these foolish divergences are comparable to a quarrel by kindergarten children on a subject like higher mathematics.

So few people today seem to realize that the Holy Bible is a collection of books by many authors. So few today are able, let alone versed in an understanding of parables and symbols. So few even suspect that there is still a deeper wisdom, hidden in certain parts of the Bible, but Mayans know this.

A smattering of science often leads to a Sunday supplement sort of an opinion concerning ancient beliefs and ideas. A materialistic sort of person never enters into the higher realms of science but often someone is called a scientist by the newspapers, because he peers earnestly through a telescope or occasionally holds a test-tube in his hand.

Among the real men of science, to name only a few who have expressed themselves for religion and miracles, I list: Kirtley F. Mather, professor of Geology, Harvard University; Heber D. Curtis, director of the Detroit observatory of the University of Michigan; Edwin G. Conklin, professor of Zoology, Princeton University; George Thomas White Patrick, professor of Philosophy, the University of Iowa; William McDougall, professor of Psychology, Duke University; Sir J. Arthur Thompson, author of "The Outline of Science," etc.; Harlan T. Stetson, director of Perkins Observatory, Ohio Wesleyan University; Sir Oliver Lodge, Dr. Robert Milliken, Dr. J. Malcolm Bird, Dr. Albert Einstein and Dr. Alexis Carrel.

Dr. Carrel started his study of Miracles through prayer in 1902. He became interested in prayer-healing because he felt that no physician was truly capable unless he studied this mode of healing as well as medicine and surgery. At that time it was dangerous for a young doctor's future career to be known to study such a subject.

Today all this is considerably changed. At Lourdes, France, a great healing center exists where any physician may observe the patients and examine the records kept in the Medical Bureau. In fact, at this place an International Medical Association of many members maintain a center. A large literature is steadily growing on the subject of miraculous healing while physicians are becoming more and more interested in the extraordinary facts.

Dr. Carrel himself says:

"Prayer should be understood, not as a mechanical recitation of formulas, but as a mystical elevation, an absorption of consciousness in the **contemplation of a principle both permeating and transcending** our world. Such a psychological state is not necessarily purely intellectual. It is incomprehensible to philosophers and scientists . . . But one must seem to feel God as easily as the heat of the sun or the kindness of a friend. The prayer which is followed by organic effects is of a special nature . . . Man offers himself to God. He stands before Him like the canvas before the painter or the marble before the sculptor. At the same time he asks for His grace, exposes his needs and those of his brothers in suffering.

"Generally, the patient who is cured is not praying for himself, but for another. Such a type of prayer demands complete renunciation—that is, a higher form of asceticism. The modest, the uneducated, and the poor seem more capable of this self-denial than the rich . . . When it possesses such characteristics, prayer may set in motion a strange phenomenon, the Miracle.

"In all the countries, at all times, people have believed in the existence of Miracles, in the more or less rapid healing of the sick at places of pilgrimage, at certain sanctuaries. But after the great impetus of science during the nineteenth century, such belief completely disappeared. It was generally admitted, not only that Miracles did not exist, but that they could not exist. As the laws of thermo-dynamics make perpetual motion impossible, physiological laws oppose miracles. Such is still the attitude of most physiologists and physicians. However, in view of the facts observed during the last fifty years, **this attitude cannot be sustained** . . . Our present conception of the influence of Prayer upon pathological lesions is based upon the observation of patients who have been cured almost **instantaneously** of various affections, such as peritoneal tuberculosis, cold abscesses, osteitis, suppurating wounds, lupus, cancer, etc. The process of healing changes little from one individual to another.

"Often, an acute pain. Then a sensation of being cured. In a few·seconds, a few minutes, at most a few hours, wounds are cicatrized, pathological symptoms disappear, appetite returns. Sometimes functional disorders vanish before the anatomical lesions are repaired. The skeletal deformations of Pott's disease, the cancerous glands, may still persist several days after the healing of the main lesions. The Miracle is chiefly characterized by an extreme acceleration of the processes of organic repair.

"There is no doubt that the rate of cicatrization of the anatomical defect is much greater than the normal one. **The only condition indispensable to the occurrence of the phenomenon is prayer.**

"But there is no need for the patient himself to pray, or even to have any religious faith. It is sufficient that someone around him be in a state of prayer. Such facts are of profound significance. They show the reality of certain relations, of still unknown nature, between psychological and organic processes. They prove the objective importance of the spiritual activities which hygienists, physicians, educators and sociologists have almost always neglected to study. They open to man a new world."

While our experience does not agree exactly with all of Dr. Carrel's findings, we feel that in the main he has considerably understated the full story that could be told.

Take the case of the brave little Band known as "The Borrowed Timers." Made up solely of people whose physicians had given them up, they lived on, far past the time predicted for them, and for several years after they were organized did not experience a single death, and in fact, only called a physician once.

Here is an entire community, each one of whom had a case history of tremendous interest to any sincere investigative body. Or, consider our daily mail with its accounts of sight restored, tumors dissolving, cancers disappearing and many other results equally miraculous, but in fields far removed from healing. Those who subscribe to our publication, Daily Meditation, read each month of many Miracles, not only of healing, but in every department of human needs.

Indeed there is a wonderful power abroad in the land— THE MIRACLE POWER. The Power you possess in dormant form, but which you may activate for anything you want through the triune transmitters, of Creative Imagination, Faith and Prayer. ANYTHING! God's power is not limited. Nothing is difficult with Him. His greatest gift is yours for the effort of asking in Faith, visualizing in Faith and making the Prayer of Faith.

For by these do you receive The Miracle Power. . .

Chapter VI

"What Things Soever Ye Desire"

WE ARE DEEPLY GRATEFUL to Dr. Carrel for his open-minded, truly scientific attitude toward miracles. Recognized as one of the ten greatest scientists, we are aware of the courage this required of him as a young doctor back in 1902. That "the psychological state necessary for miracles is incomprehensible to philosophers," we must however, deny. And we feel that the denial demands no proof in that it was the great philosophers of all ages who gave the Laws that govern the appearance of The Miracle Power.

That all men do not succeed in always accomplishing the Miracles does not disprove that it works as a Law. All men could apply the rules of addition, but when some get the wrong total that does not disprove mathematics. Nor does man's open, **or private** lack of faith disprove the law of The Miracle Power.

For few indeed are those who actually, both **inwardly** and outwardly, BELIEVE the plain teachings of the greatest Miracle Maker among men. He stated the law repeatedly and in many varied phrasings. It was written down by several of His Apostles. It appears in all the Gospels. It has been read by tens,—yes, hundreds of thousands of humankind. Yet only a few have been able to call forth the Miracles. Only a few

hundred thousand from among teeming millions through
two thousands of years have demonstrated that they were
free,—totally free from doubts. Why? Because, like the aver
age philosopher they were filled with questionings.

Many have **professed** their belief. But they had doubt in
their hearts. They struggled to believe by assuring themselves
with words, but privately they did not have the Faith, and
without Faith, miracles are dead. But with a consciousness
freed from doubting, Miracles occur, just as wonderful, just
as spectacular, just as miraculous as ever. This is most veril*
the Truth. And,

"THE TRUTH SHALL MAKE YE FREE"

Through the centuries many good men of the cloth have
explained what "Jesus meant" when He said thus and so
So few have taught that He meant exactly what He said
John reported His words rigidly, absolutely correctly when
he wrote down that the Master said:

"Verily, verily, I say unto **you,**
He that believeth on me
THE WORKS THAT I DO SHALL YE DO ALSO
AND GREATER WORKS THAN THESE SHALL YE DO.*
John 14:12.

The meaning intended by these words is clear. There i
no possibility of our doubting what He meant if we will onl*
realize that they are True. There are no qualifying word
that were left out. Jesus knew that even as He uttered the
words, as He gave out the secret, that for the most part the*
believed Him not. No philosopher who will understand tha
THIS is a statement of the Law of the Miracle Power, nor an*
other man or woman, need ever fail to get results. But one
must understand what the words say. He must realize the
terrible earnestness of The Savior when He sought to impres
His listeners by repeating the affirmative, "VERILY, VERILY*
I SAY UNTO YOU." Then He states the Law, "HE THA*

BELIEVETH," and the final miraculous promise made just after He had performed a great number of the most astonishing miracles,

"THE WORKS THAT I DO SHALL YE DO ALSO,—and GREATER Works Than These Shall Ye Do."

But ever since, as ever before, man has stubbornly, or perhaps I should say, modestly, refused to believe that he too can perform miracles, even though the very next words Jesus spoke were:

"And WHATSOEVER Ye Shall Ask In My Name, That Will I Do."

Surely this should be enough to convince anyone that he has a special gift, a power to call upon for any worthy purpose, that will not fail him. But if it is NOT enough His next words were:

"If Ye Ask ANYTHING In My Name, That Will I Do."

You will find all this in your family Bible, by turning to John, the 14th Chapter, Verses 12, 13, and 14. You have the word of Scripture for it. Jesus tells you that "Whatsoever" ye ask and "Anything" you ask, and tells you that you can do things such as He did and even more marvelous things. All that is necessary is that you BELIEVE, that you be FREE FROM DOUBT.

True, He was talking to His disciples when He said these things. But YOU can be a disciple of Christ too, if you will. That does not necessarily mean that you will have to greatly change your present life,—that is, providing your present life is not an evil one. If it were, it is not very likely that you would be greatly interested in reading these words. So for you, it is probably only necessary that you change your thoughts and that the little adjustments to make your life more worthy will follow without your even trying very hard.

Jesus' next words cover this and give directions and state His idea of what is expected of a Disciple when He says:

"If Ye LOVE Me, Ye Will Keep My Commandments."

That is really all that is required for Discipleship,— Love. It is not usually difficult to love one who is so loving that He offers ANYTHING you ask, or who says, "Whatsoever Ye Ask, That Will I Do." How could one have such a friend, such a kindly companion and not love him?

The trouble is that most of us think of Christ as being dead. We think of ourselves as existing only in the mortal body. We, without thought, are half conscious of previous lives but think of this one as the last. We are aware that everything in the physical world has a beginning and an end and we live as though our being was a thing wholly physical instead of realizing that we are also Spirit, Mind and Soul. We mouth the word "Immortal" but think of death as being the end.

That is not true.

"YOU AND THE FATHER ARE ONE."

The very word "ONE" is from an ancient symbol of The Maya, a symbol doubtless thousands of years old when Christ Jesus was born. Its meaning is this:

God is All. There is only one All. If there were more than one All, it would not be All. Therefore, God is One; The All.

GOD IS ALL and ALL IS ONE.

All, is Complete, Unity, Oneness. You are a part of The All.

The first letter of the word "One" is an ancient Mayan symbol for eternity. Eternity is without beginning or end. The circle of the letter "O" best expresses this thought because it too, when completed, has no end. So sacred was this symbol of the circle in ancient days among the Maya, that, with rare exceptions it was never used, except in connection with the most sacred rites, the most sacred mysteries or in the most sacred temples. So sacred was it that even wheels were forbidden for common usage, or for wagons or carts even though roads and highways built by these people tens of centuries ago are still serviceable; even though they practiced an extensive commerce and traveled far. Even in the ancient Mayan writings, when the circle symbol was used it was drawn imperfectly as it was believed that man should not attempt to portray the perfection of God, the All, the One.

How much more noble is this great and grand conception of One All-God, The Great Spirit, than the European dark-ages idea of a Man sitting on a throne, invisible, far off, surrounded by clouds and cherubim playing harps through eternity. With such a vision well in mind, is it any wonder that people try to hide their deeds from Him, to deceive Him, and to fear Him?

God, the Creator, is a God of Love. He is the Father of Love and Life and Joy and Abundance. The Father is in You. He is in Everything and Everything is within Him, the One, the All. As you are conscious of your acts, your thoughts, your deeds, so is He who is All Consciousness also aware of them.

He is aware of You, in His All-Wisdom. It is We, who in our smallness too often are not aware of Him.

Then, start now to become aware of His constant presence within you and all about you. Become aware and understand that "You and The Father **ARE** One." Free your mind of doubts. Know that His Powers are Within you awaiting only for you to call upon them. Learn the Truth and apply it to your own religion whatever it may be. The Truth shall make you Free. Free from fear, from unhappiness, from doubt, from lack, from all the limitations and privations produced through lack of Understanding. BELIEVE in The Miracle Power.

Read the whole chapter of John 14 from your Bible. They are the last words of Jesus as He prepared to go to His physical death,—the death He had predicted and foretold. Would any man, going to his doom, speak insincerely? How much less would this wise and gentle leader. His last words repeating over and over in varying phraseology the same message of the availability of Miracles to you and me, to all of us, if we will but ask in Faith.

There is a magnificent comfort in Truth, once you understand it. And Jesus knew this too, and spoke of it to His friends gathered together there. He said:

"And I will pray the Father, and He shall give you another comforter, that he may be with you forever, even the Spirit of Truth; **whom the world cannot receive,** for it beholdeth him not, neither knoweth him; **Ye know him;** for he abideth **with** you, and shall be **in** you.

I will not leave you desolate: I come unto you. Yet a little while, and the world beholdeth me no more, **but ye behold me:** because I live, ye shall live also. **In that Day Ye Shall Know That I Am In My Father, and Ye In Me, and I In You."**

John 14: 16 to 20.

Then once more He repeated again the secret that the world even today passes by. Scientists seek fruitlessly for the cause for miracles, philosophers search in vain for the **reason;** but one who has Faith needs neither cause nor reason. For him, all that is necessary is that he have Faith and his needs, regardless of their nature, are fulfilled. In John 15:7 we find again the promise when Jesus says:

"If ye abide in me, and my words abide in you, **ask whatsoever ye will,** and it shall be done unto you."

But even after this, the disciples wondered and still failed to understand and were filled with questionings. Even they missed the message. Small wonder that the world fails to receive the Spirit of Truth, when even His disciples after repeated speakings of the secret failed to note it.

So **twice** more Jesus patiently gave them again the simple directions for invoking the Miracle Power. A means so simple, so easy to do, that the world passes it by. His words this time were:

"Verily, Verily, I say unto you, if ye ask ANYTHING of the Father, He will give it to you in my name."

and

"Hitherto have ye asked nothing in my name: ASK, and ye SHALL receive, that your joy may be made full."

One would think that these plain words would finally be understood clearly by all those present. But let me ask YOU a question:

Have they yet convinced **you?** Can you place yourself through your mentality, there in that little group; can you feel in your heart just a little of the kindly Jesus' anguish in parting with those whom He loved; can you sense His tremendous earnestness as He tried to impress upon them the availability of The Miracle Power of God? Listen to His next words and decide in your heart if they were not also meant for YOU:

"These things have I spoken unto you in dark sayings: the hour cometh, when I shall no more speak unto you in dark sayings, but shall tell you plainly of the Father. In that day ye shall ask in my name: and I say not unto you, that I will pray the Father for you; **for the Father Himself Loveth You,** because ye have loved me, and have believed that I came forth from the Father."

Is this the age when we need no more to speak in parables, in dark sayings? Is this the age when His word is finally to be understood? Is this the time when the Spirit of Truth shall come to you?

"Howbeit when he, the Spirit of Truth, is come, he shall guide you into All the Truth: for he shall not speak from himself; but what things soever he shall hear, these shall he speak: and he shall declare unto you the things that are to come.

"He shall glorify me: for he shall take of mine, and shall declare it unto you.

"All things whatsoever the Father hath are mine: therefore sayeth I, that he taketh of mine, and shall declare it unto you."

Things spoken of darkly? Yes, but plainly, if you will but understand these things.

1.   That, God is All and All is God.
2.   That, you are a very part of Him.
3.   That, His Miraculous Powers are within you, as you are within Him and that "whatsoever the Father hath" is yours, **just as all that you possess is also His.**
4.   That, you need only ask in Faith, doubting not in your heart, to receive ANYTHING you NEED.

"And Jesus answering saith unto them, Have Faith in God. Verily I say unto you, **Whosoever** shall say unto this mountain, Be thou taken up and cast into the sea; **and shall not doubt in his heart, but shall believe that what he saith cometh to pass; He Shall Have It!**

"Therefore I say unto YOU,
All things whatsoever ye pray and ask for,
Believe that Ye Receive them,
And YE SHALL have them."

THERE IS A GUIDING LIGHT LEADING YOU

Chapter VII

The Great Brotherhood

INBORN in every man and in every woman is a something
that tends to draw together those of like minds or like
tastes. We read in the daily papers of the meetings of
Scientific Societies, of religious groups, of this and that
organization of people who are attracted mentally by
similar things.

Nor is this a phenomenon but rather an innate recognition that here among this group we will find kindred
minds and understanding souls. It is the instinct which led
man upward, away from savagery, the instinct which created great cities and nations, great Universities and schools.
It, more than any other trait perhaps, is responsible for
civilization's great advancement, indeed for civilization itself. This instinct is an expression of Divine Love, when in
its higher manifestations, and a sub-conscious recognition
of the Brotherhood of Man.

We see it in great organizations, in great fraternal
orders and in secret Wisdom Societies all over the world.
And in this manifestation we believe it has its greatest opportunity.

Drawn together by a desire for strange mystic knowledge of man's powers and the wish to improve their lives,

many men and women have joined the Mayan Order in North America. Unlike the Masonic Order and other fraternal orders possessing and teaching ancient esoteric wisdom, The Mayans receive both men and women in full and equal membership. Both husband and wife may join. This fraternal Order which draws its teachings from ancient and modern philosophies has spread so rapidly through the years that today its members are in every part of the North American continent.

. Members are permitted to ask others to join the Mayan Order, but one must seek admittance. Rarely, someone is officially invited to join because of some special aptness or for some other reason. Among those who have been so invited, are world famous persons. Those who do seek and gain admittance do so only by submitting certain data concerning themselves and by a vote of the Order's Membership Committee. To be a Mayan is considered a signal honor and an indication that you are judged to possess some outstanding ability.

Once a Mayan, a Mayan Always, has long been the slogan among those who receive "the word." It is a Companionship that is very important and very real among the members, even though they seldom meet face to face. Instructions, lessons, monographs, various publications are received at regular intervals every month by each member without any price being placed upon them, and all members are proud of the good works performed by the Order, the research among the pyramids of Central America, and the very real service extended without charge to their community by each Mayan.

Not least among Mayan activities is the Chapel of Miracles used by members and non-members. Each month hundreds of people write to the Mayan Order asking that we pray with them as they submit their written prayers. Many thousands have sent their written prayers to be placed in the Chapel of Miracles described before. You, as a reader of this book, are also invited to do so whenever you have a need.

And to this place, three times each day, all Mayans everywhere, turn their attention in prayerful Meditation. Miracles by the score have been reported as the result of prayer under this direction.

Indeed the manner of carrying on the work of the Chapel of Miracles is itself a sort of miracle. It is self-supporting, yet no charge is ever made for services. Despite the fact that in one year the Order used radio time over the then most powerful radio station in the world, and ministered to all the many thousands who responded to these nation-wide broadcasts, purchasing tons of paper and thousands of stamps, and giving away thousands of booklets, no charge was ever made. Despite all this tremendous expense, — a way was always provided. Like the oil from the widow's cruse, the money came through Faith in the Giver of all good.

This is comparable to the work of George Muller who, in England, maintained orphanages which spent millions, through which hundreds were rescued from the slums and fitted for places of trust in the world—all without any visible means of support! Many and many a time utter penury stared George Muller in the face, so that any man of less Job-like Faith would have been discouraged. Once, hundreds of hungry children sat waiting for their breakfast—and there was not a mouthful to give them.

But always in time—though sometimes at the very last minute—his faith was justified and some generous donation would supply all their wants.

The luminous crosses that shone in the dark from thousands of bed-room walls in America were made by the group of people known as "The Borrowed Timers," and is another miraculous demonstration of Faith fulfilled.

Wishing to be useful in this life, they made these luminous crosses that glowed in the dark as a reminder of prayer and the Miracles that come through prayer. By this means alone, they were self-supporting.

Faith makes these miracles. Faith and the spreading of Faith to others. We grow by living and we live by growing.

"ALL THAT THE FATHER HATH IS YOURS"
"THERE IS NO LACK IN HIM IN WHOM ALL
FULLNESS LIES."

What is your Need? Is it money? Then realize that God is the source of all wealth. So go to Him—tell Him your need—ask Him for money in abundance to meet your needs. Bless the money you **now** have,—**put it to some good work**—remember what Jesus did with the loaves and fishes—how they MULTIPLIED,—do that with the money you now have—not by hoarding it, but by putting it into action, in some good work. Use it to develop Character, Culture and Friendships.

WHAT should you do to make it multiply?

Ask Him what you should do. Ask the Father to direct you, to lead your thoughts that you may know what you should do. Then DO it—in FAITH.

Wherever you are and whatever you need, supply is always there. There is no lack in the Universe. Supply is in the Father, and the Father is everywhere. The supply is not far off, it's like the air we breathe—it is all around us, always available, always plentiful,—unless we have doubt in our hearts—only by this are we limited. Health, happiness, prosperity, ANY need can be fulfilled through the Father.

There are really only two kinds of prayerful people in the world. One kind prays only in some dire emergency. He only prays when he wants something and wants it badly and quickly. If his prayer is not answered he says, "Prayer doesn't work." If his prayer, because of his urgency, is answered, he forgets about it until the next great emergency. Sometimes he is not even decently thankful.

The other kind is the sort Jesus meant when He admonished us to "pray without ceasing." That doesn't mean to spend our whole lives on our knees beseeching. It does mean to think prayerful thoughts often, to live the good life, to seek the Father in prayer every day, in privacy, to devote certain times to prayerful Meditation. Only by Meditative thought does any person develop mentally. A daily practice of Meditation works wonders not only for your Mind, but for your body, Spirit and Soul.

Old Mother Nature follows the practice of daily communion with the Creator. The flowers turn their faces to the sun, not just once a day, or once a week,—but always. The grain, the shrubs, the trees, the grass, drink in the life and light of the sun every day and all day. They receive the communion as often and as long as opportunity affords.

And that is what you should do too. First, know exactly what it is you need or want. Then pray for it, seek it earnestly and continuously, **with faith that you ARE RECEIVING** it and **without doubt in your heart.**

The habit of taking a little time daily, alone in the quiet, in communion with one's Source—that the illumination and guidance of the Holy Spirit may become alive and active in your life; and going about one's daily work happily and ever open to, and conscious of, this Divine Presence and Power; will bring definiteness and direction—will bring hope and courage; will bring Peace and Power to EVERYONE WHO DOES IT.

In ancient days the Mayan Angelus Call was made at morning, mid-day and night by ringing a great silver gong-like bell. Originally this was rung at the rising of the sun, at mid-day, and at the setting of the sun. The sun, mightiest of the stars, was long ago accepted by the wise men as an appropriate symbol of the Almighty One.

In present day Mayanry, ministering over a large part of the earth's surface, we give the Angelus Call thrice daily as has always been the custom, but in order that all may have the opportunity of uniting their prayers with all the others observing this rite at the same moment, the Call is now given at 9:00 A.M., at 3:00 P.M., and at 9:00 P.M., Central Standard Time.

Readers of this book will gladly be given the exact schedule for observance of The Angelus Call in the part of the country in which they live by writing to The Mayan Order, Box 2710, San Antonio 6, Texas. Further information is to be found in a booklet published by the Order, entitled "How To Pray." This book may be had without charge by writing to The Mayans and enclosing a nominal sum to cover the cost of sending it to you. No charge is made, send what you please, to be devoted to furthering the Order's work.

You are also invited to send your written prayer to be placed in the Prayer-Room of Miracles. We will gladly place it there and pray with you at the time of the Angelus. Your written prayer will remain there for thirty days and at the end of this time we ask that you notify us of the results you have obtained.   If you wish, you may then renew your written prayer for another thirty day period and continue to renew it until your prayer is answered.

Some prayers are fulfilled quickly, even instantaneously, while others, because of their nature, require more time. But regardless of the length of time no charge is ever made for prayer.   The Prayer Room is maintained by the free-will and love offerings of those who call upon it for its services.

A written prayer is often found to be a more effective form of prayer for a number of reasons.   Chiefly, it calls for a better concentration of thought than many are able to give in a spoken prayer, and provides more definiteness of direction for the desires we have.   Like the focusing of a spot-light, or the rays of the sun through a glass, we should focus our desires and our attention in prayer.

"ALL THAT THE FATHER HATH IS YOURS"

What do you seek?   Try, earnestly, writing a prayer. Then:

Send it to The Prayer Room, ...

Chapter VIII

How To Manifest The Miracle Power

THE MIRACLE POWER, as we have learned, is the Power of God dwelling within us. If it is His Power and He is All, then it is All-Power and cannot fail. It is as eternal and as powerful as God Himself because it IS the Power of God Himself.

The Miracle Power does not fail,—if we do not get results through its use, it is because WE fail in some way and prevent its manifesting. The Father is desirous of helping us, of providing the way for us to bring about anything that we need or desire. We have read Jesus' last words, actually pleading that we ask ANYTHING we want.

The trouble is, we are so accustomed to thinking of man's feeble powers.—We think of our limitations instead of our freedoms. We think, "My, how my head aches," instead of thinking of the glorious BLESSINGS we possess.— Yet who among us have not had a headache vanish—when we had our attention diverted to something else.

God made us with a nervous system—so that we might be warned when through some wrong act we endangered the mechanism of our body.—He did not make us so that pain was the normal thing. He made us so that pain is abnormal. WE MAKE THE CONDITION THAT CAUSES PAIN,

AND WE MAKE THE PAIN WORSE BY DIRECTING OUR ATTENTION TO IT . . . Instead of to Him and the Image of Perfection, and we do the same thing when we bend our attention to poverty and lack.

Think, "my head aches," and it DOES ache. Think of PERFECTION instead of the ache in your head and the ache is gone,—until you think of it again.

I do not mean, half think of "perfection." I mean FILL your Mind with it . . . think of it rapturously, joyously, completely, shutting out ALL OTHER THOUGHTS and your head CAN'T ache. You see you must give ATTENTION to pain to experience pain.

Perhaps you have had an experience like this or know someone who has:

There was an automobile accident. One minute the driver was sitting in his car, going along fifty miles an hour, and perfectly all right. Suddenly a car shoots out from a side road—there is a collision, flying glass, a terrific noise, and—darkness.—No pain.—None whatsoever. There was no time to think pain before unconsciousness took place. But hours later, in the hospital when consciousness returned,—there was time to think pain and pain was there.

So you see the principle is simple . . . It is Understanding that is difficult to get . . . With some, Understanding comes instantly and they start to demonstrate right away. With others, it comes more slowly, and with some,—Understanding in its complete sense is never attained.

But Understanding, though desirable, is not essential to use this principle. All that is necessary is FAITH.

"A FAITH THAT SURPASSETH UNDERSTANDING WORKS INSTANT MIRACLES TO PERFORM."

Do not struggle to attain FAITH, for the struggle will lock it out. Simply BELIEVE and if you will, strive to UNDERSTAND.

If at the start your FAITH is small, it must not be forced, but instead, it should be cultivated—slowly and reasonably, yet constantly.

Each day you should devote some time to Meditation upon the teachings in this book . . . until Understanding and Belief grow to maturity in definite Knowledge.—And as your Knowledge grows and ripens, FAITH brings forth the fruit which is WISDOM.

But never struggle for Faith. Never say, "I am well" while some part of you denies it, saying privately, "I am sick." Such divided Faith is unproductive. Instead, say "I am GETTING well." You need not struggle to BELIEVE that.

THIS IS IMPORTANT! . . . Let your Faith be single and sincere . . . without worrying or fearing that that which you desire may not be. Do not struggle for Faith . . . Do not strive for it. Simply image in your Mind the Perfection of your desires. Be confident that God has all the Power needed, and that He does answer Prayers . . . and that YOU are made in His image.

Instead of creating castles in the air—instead of day dreaming—instead of just sitting back and idly asking God to do all your work; instead of this, go out and work to bring it about yourself. Work in confidence that you will succeed. Work in the certain knowledge that you in His Image are a Creator too. Ask in Faith, then Act in Faith. "PICK UP THY BED AND WALK."

Realize and remember always, if you seek new understanding, that God is not some man sitting somewhere on a cloud, far off. He is not a SHAPE like mortal man, nor man of a SHAPE like Him. The image and likeness are the invisible Creative POWERS, the IMAGING ability we possess.

The shape of our physical bodies is mortal. The image is GOD-LIKE and IMMORTAL.

Instead of thinking of God as some very old, far away and wrathful man, think of Him as Life. Life is in everything that is. And so is God ever Present. And Life is intelligent. Anyone who has planted a seed and watched it grow knows that.

Anyone capable of thinking, who has witnessed the miracle of birth and growth recognizes that. Anyone who has watched life seek the light recognizes the kinship of that impulse with something deep inside himself which yearns toward Illumination, toward the good and the Perfect and the Powerful.

And as we receive the Light of Illumination into our intellects, so do we ever more Image perfection until we BECOME in that Image ourselves.

GOD IS ALL
and
ALL IS GOD
AND GOD IS ALL ABOUT YOU.
BELIEVE THAT, AND LIGHT WILL ENTER
INTO YOU!

There are few who . . . reading these thoughts for the first time, will understand them perfectly. Do not be discouraged if that is your experience. If they were easy to understand without thought and without study, you would have no need for them. If you find them strange and difficult . . . that only proves your great need for them. People who reject the strange never progress, never learn and never benefit. It is only those who explore new fields of thought who develop.

Your past thinking makes you what you are today. If you were satisfied with that condition you would not be reading these words.

It is your recognition of your need for better things that has led you to these words. These teachings have brought miracles to others. They can do as much or even more for you.

BUT A SINGLE CASUAL READING WILL NOT SUFFICE IF YOU ARE TO GET ALL POSSIBLE BENEFIT FROM THIS BOOK.

At first you may be inclined to reject parts of it. Later, after you have studied a while, you will come back to this book and discover new Truths. Remember this System of Thought HAS produced results that can only properly be termed . . . MIRACLES.

IT IS IMPORTANT THEREFORE THAT YOU DECIDE NOW THAT YOU WILL MAKE THIS MIRACLE POWER PRINCIPLE WORK FOR YOU TOO. SET YOUR MIND FIRMLY IN THE ABSOLUTE DETERMINATION—THAT IF ALL THAT IS NECESSARY TO CHANGE CONDITIONS ABOUT YOU IS TO CHANGE YOUR HABITS OF THINKING, THAT THEN YOU **WILL** CHANGE YOUR THINKING HABITS AND RECEIVE ALL OF THE THINGS YOU DESIRE.

When Aladdin received the wonderful lamp told of in fable, he still had to rub it and then tell the genie WHAT it was he wanted. If he had not BELIEVED the genie would appear,—he would never have performed the simple act of rubbing the lamp.

AND SO IT IS WITH YOU!

You must first BELIEVE. Then you must follow our directions. Make up your mind that the year ahead **will** be different for you. Then stay with that determination and do what is required of you. And continue to do it until results come for you too. Continue at least for the next twelve months and you will find your life tremendously improved in every way. I guarantee this, fully.

AND REMEMBER ALWAYS THAT THE MIRACLE POWER, THE DIVINE CREATIVE PRINCIPLE, WORKS MIRACULOUSLY, EVEN AFTER EVERYTHING ELSE HAS FAILED.

One thing more should be explained here briefly, before you are ready to start. That is concerning the principle behind the use of "affirmations." An Affirmation is an avowal of Faith directed in a certain Path or Image. It is a key to unlock Hidden God-Given POWERS YOU POSSESS.

We learn from the science of psychology that man possesses a dual mentality. He has a conscious mind and a sub-conscious mind. This is now so generally accepted that we have no need to go into it in detail here. Suffice to say that the sub-conscious receives impulses from the conscious mind. When these impulses are received in the sub-conscious it accepts them WITHOUT QUESTION.

Therefore when you hold a thought strongly in your consciousness, whether it be good or ill, when it finally penetrates into your sub-conscious—it becomes a fact so far as the workings of your body are concerned.

Believe and hold the thought that you are ill and you become ill. Believe and hold the thought that you are well and healthy and you become well and healthy.

Both beliefs are forms of Creative Imaging. One is negative thinking . . . the other, positive. But the Principle works both ways.

This provides the clue to one of the physical powers of the use of Affirmations. In this way, we add to the Power of Prayer, the Power of Affirmations.

In using affirmations, repeat them often. Repeat them many, many times. Repeat them WITHOUT any struggle to believe. Without any struggle for Faith. Simply repeat the ones applicable to your needs many, many times each day. By thus repeating them consciously without thoughts of doubt, but inwardly beholding PERFECTION, they soon penetrate to the sub-consciousness—whereupon the Image becomes reality.

The daily practice of Meditation is an attunement with your Maker. It is the means of developing the intellect and ennobling our minds. NO intellectual development is possible without it, even if we are unaware that we are practicing it. The conscious, intentional, and REGULAR practice of Meditation daily is the direct road to Mental Mastery. It is a means within everyone's reach. It does not require high education nor demand a super-mind to do it.

Yet it is the means by which our super-mental development occurs. And that is something we, all of us, like to have.

Daily Meditation brings us into daily communion with our Supreme Father. It provides an inspiring nearness to Him. And we get out of this practice exactly what we put into it—multiplied.

A new student once said:—"It has been wonderful during the past few minutes of my Meditation. If only I could know how to keep this blessed nearness to my Master that I feel just now, I would be the happiest person in the world."

I replied:—"I will tell you how to do it. Spend fifteen minutes every day TALKING TO GOD IN PRAYER . . . fifteen minutes every day LETTING God TALK TO YOU through Meditation AND fifteen minutes every day talking ABOUT God to someone else."

Dear Reader of this Book and Seeker of Better Things, DO that . . . do it every day and I promise that you will be amazed by the quick results you get.

Memorize affirmations that are most helpful to you. Repeat them many times, aloud . . . or as a whisper, or mentally. Meditate much upon them. They will be food to your Soul, Light to your Pathway, and weapons for your warfare.

Put on the armor of God and devote time every day to Meditation and Prayer and you will soon come to Understand that Heaven is here on earth if we will see The Light.

This practice followed even for only a few months will have a saving, ennobling, transforming influence NOT ONLY UPON YOU, BUT UPON ALL ABOUT YOU. Great thoughts, perfect health, noble aspirations, clear perceptions of Truth and duty to God, and much gain may be yours.

"Thy word is a lamp unto my feet and light unto my path . . ."

119th Psalm, 105th Verse

New Daily Meditations are issued each month by the Mayans and contain a thought for each day of the month and affirmations designed to cover all human needs. You may obtain this private monthly publication called "D.M." for a FULL YEAR for only $4.00. The year's supply is equal in size and volume to ten books like this, so you see it brings you a vast amount of help. You may also arrange to have it sent to any of your friends if you desire, at the same rate.

The Instructions that follow are to be used in connection with your Daily Meditations. The Miracle Power does not require long laborious study in order to use it. It only needs regular Meditation and application of the principle. If you are of a scientific trend of mind, or like Solomon, seek the deeper understanding, that, too, you may attain.

If you desire that . . . we suggest you ask for a Membership in the Mayan Order. Our province is that of a Guiding Light leading you—toward that which you seek.

"Ask and ye shall receive, seek and ye shall find. Knock and it shall be opened unto you."

As you advance on The Path that Destiny has placed before you, as you learn to hearken to that Inner Light which guides your steps, be diligent in observing the daily regime.

A Prayer that is only thought of, scarcely breathed even—while you continue at your work, if it is offered in Faith, is more valuable than ten thousand words without Faith.

Know this—that according to your Faith you are AL-READY RECEIVING. And according to the Image of your desire it will materialize. If you use this Miracle Power and gain only one important objective, you have benefited a hundred-fold, but use it in all your affairs, and you gain the Kingdom of Heaven right here on earth. Heaven is not a place, it is a condition. Use the daily Affirmations DAILY. They are the essence of the Principle that Creates.

Chapter IX

Special Guidance

On Various Problems To Be Used In Connection With
Appropriate Daily Lessons And Meditations

HOW TO RECEIVE HELP TO CHOOSE A DEFINITE MAJOR AIM IN LIFE:

Send for The Order's book entitled "How to Pray." It is free. Read it carefully. At the Angelus Calls, ask God to reveal to you which Path you should choose to follow as your Major Aim in Life. ASK! Then LISTEN FOR HIS ANSWER. Let your Mind be passive, open to new thoughts and **Wait** FOR HIS ANSWER.

It may come as a sudden enlightening decision—that will brook no doubting. It may come into your consciousness as a series of enlightening pictures. It may come to you as a sudden startling revelation.

Wait for His answer! Go back to God many times with this question if necessary until His answer comes into your Mind.

HOW TO FIND ASSISTANCE FOR CREATING THE RIGHT PLAN TO ACQUIRE THE OBJECT OF YOUR PURPOSE:

Do exactly as you have been instructed above. Talk it over with God exactly as you would with your earthly father. But remember that with God—you are much nearer than you ever could be with any earthly father.

He knows your most secret thoughts. YOU can conceal nothing of your secret purpose from Him. HIS powers and forces flow through you and are in you and all about you. You are a living part of Him. For HE IS ALL.

Talk it over with your Almighty Father—and wait for His Revelation of the Plan to reveal itself in your consciousness.

HOW TO RECEIVE DAILY DIRECTIONS FOR UNLOCKING HIDDEN MYSTERIOUS POWERS WITHIN YOU:

Anything you desire in Faith that is worthy, you may have. There are millions of reflections of the One Great Divine Creative Principle. Many applications of this are given to you in the Daily Meditations. One should not be content to merely read these. One should Meditate upon them. As a daily practice one should Meditate upon not only the thoughts given to you in the daily lessons, but upon the thoughts these bring forth.

Meditate often . . . upon the glory of God and His absolute constant nearness to you.

HOW TO TRAIN ONESELF TO MENTAL ATTUNEMENT WITH THE ALL-POWER:

God is ALL. Therefore He is also ALL POWER. There is nothing beyond the ALL. You are a Part of All. If you were not you would be nothing. As you ARE something you are a part of ALL. You are therefore a part of God who is ALL.

His Mind is the ALL-MIND. YOUR Mind is part of His Mind, the All-Mind. You are therefore attuned to His Mind Now. God gives us the Freedom of Individuality. To be conscious of your attunement with Him, drop your individuality and submerge yourself in the Allness of the ALL. FEEL His Greatness encompassing your Being. That IS ATTUNEMENT!

HOW TO STIR UP COURAGE AND NERVE TO DEMAND MORE OUT OF LIFE AND GET IT:

Courage and "nerve" are merely confidence and Freedom from Fear. Realize that God Himself and His All-Power and All-Mind are within you as part of the All. With the realization that all this power and all this mentality are yours to call upon and to use, you will be filled with courage and confidence.

It is yours to call upon, yours to use and you are learning more surely each day, how to call upon it and how to put it into use so that you will demand more out of life, and get it. Learn the way of Affirmations during the year ahead.

HOW YOU MAY HAVE AT YOUR CALL A TREMENDOUS FORCE FOR GETTING ANYTHING YOU WANT FROM LIFE:

"In FAITH all things are possible." Through Faith, as you will come to learn, many powers now dwelling dormant within you are unleashed and your abilities develop. In any effort, first BELIEVE that you can, Meditate upon how you will do it, talk it over with God, then start DOING IT. Keep in mind always, that you are not alone. God is with you constantly. Each day as you join your thoughts with the thousands in all parts of the North American Continent, you are not alone.

In United Thought there is Strength. In United Petitioning to the Throne of Grace, there is communion with God. In Meditation there is Power. Practice it daily. Develop the ability to Meditate upon your plans and needs deeply and sincerely. Even if you are in the midst of some other pressing activity, manage to direct a few sincere thoughts in Meditative contemplation of your needs. Keep that vision ever before you. Don't let it grow dim or hazy. And repeat as many times daily as possible, either silently or aloud, the affirmation most suitable to your needs.

HOW TO "STEP UP" YOUR OWN MENTAL POWERS AND PUT THEM INTO ACTION:

After a quiet period of Meditation, sit still for a time and direct your consciousness to your brain. Feel the refreshing magnetizing flow of Power come into it as you relax utterly for a few moments. Then tackle the problem perfectly refreshed mentally. The brain is mortal, like your body. Consciousness is immortal. Direct your consciousness and your attention to your brain for a brief quiet moment. Relax. Feel the renewed power now present. Try it! Now!

HOW TO BE LIFTED ABOVE PETTY WORRIES AND FEARS AND HAMPERING DRAGS:

Select certain of the Daily Meditation Lessons as your favorites. Memorize certain of the Affirmations given to you at the end of each Daily Meditation. Worry is merely fear and usually it is without any real basis, and fear of course is always a drag.

It is a form of expectant thinking in reverse. Then put it back in its proper place and think straight, "expectantly." We get what we expect. Have confidence in God and think expectantly the right way. FEEL His constant Loving Presence.

HOW TO GAIN A NEW AND SATISFYING HOLD ON YOUR RELIGION:

Errors in translation, and errors in the understanding of some of the ancient writers have occasionally been carried down into most of the Modern Creeds. Injunctions to "Fear God" and warnings that "Thy God is a jealous God" seem clearly to be examples of this. The original injunction was to revere God instead of to fear Him.

Whenever you find the words, "Fear God," try substituting reverence for Him and see how much it helps you to find a new satisfaction in your Religion.

An earthly father does not desire his children to stand in fear of him, but he does desire their respect.

In the higher degrees of the Mayan Order one learns so much about the original teachings and sees how they became perverted into totally different meanings during the passing of the centuries.

To gain a new and satisfying hold on your Religion, gain greater Understanding. By observance of regular periods of Meditation, come to know the very real nearness to you of the Almighty Father. Realize the kinship and recognize that He is in you and you are in Him.

In the words of Jesus, "I and the Father are One," meaning YOU AND THE FATHER ARE ONE.

Thus, you may find new Understanding of God and His Real Love for you.

HOW TO CONVERT FAILURE INTO SUCCESS:

When you think of failure, you show it in countless subtle ways that leave you open to predatory attacks. It is the way of unenlightened men to "kick a man when he is down." Those who have not seen the Light and who are filled with greed and selfishness are quick to take advantage of those whose position may be weak.

In this way and in many other ways thinking failure seems to attract failure. Likewise to think Success attracts Success.

Picture yourself as a Success and Live The Part. As you imagine yourself so will you become. The successful man is a thoughtful man who plans his moves. Do thou likewise. Take your plans to God and wait for His answer. Then BELIEVE and DO according to His Divine Directions.

If your plans are good and well thought out, and approved by God; if you Believe in them, how can you help thinking SUCCESS. Like attracts like and Success attracts Success. Hold the Affirmative Successful attitude and the world will flock to you and make you even more Successful.

Be worthy of Success and when Success starts to come give more and more and become worthy of more and more Success. You can be as successful as you choose to be.

"GIVE AND YE SHALL RECEIVE"

Give what . . . ? Give the very best you have to give. If you are a musician, give your best. If your abilities are in the field of commerce, give the best values.

If you follow law, give the best advice and representation. Whatever field you are best in, give your best in the biggest, most generous way possible and you will Succeed.

"WITH WHAT MEASURE YE METE IT OUT SO SHALL IT BE MEASURED UNTO YOU."

Keep actively doing. Give, and give, and give. And think affirmatively of Success so constantly . . . that there is no time for thinking otherwise.

By our thoughts we do create, and in the image of our thinking. Do this and you will find the Door Opened for a new approach to Spiritual as well as Material Riches. There is another door opened to you as well.

Each year, the Mayan Order accepts into their Companionship a certain number of persons who have in one way or another been selected as being worthy of this honor. This door to deeper mysteries and greater Wisdom is open to you . . . as a Reader of this book. During this year certain ones will be selected from among those who seek admission to receive the Mayan Initiation. May you be one of them!

HOW DISEASE AND ILL HEALTH MAY BE CONQUERED BY A GOD-POWER EVERY PERSON POSSESSES:

Do you feel tired in any part of your body? Do this: Direct your attention to that part of your body for a period of thirty seconds. Try this as an experiment.

Hold your attention mentally, for a brief thirty seconds on any part of your body, say your left hand or your right foot. While your attention is thus concentrated, WILL that the Life energy in your body be sent abundantly to that region. After thirty seconds, relax. But FEEL the restoration of Well Being in the member you have concentrated upon.

Try doing that . . . before you read another word beyond this point. No doubt you will be amazed at the peculiar feeling of well being and new energy in the part of your body you directed your attention to.

You see Mind DOES Control Body. Whether you are conscious of it or not, it DOES. Every second that you live in the physical body, Mind is on the job taking care of you, keeping the physical functions going. You are not conscious of it because most of these activities are taken care of by your sub-conscious mind. It keeps your heart beating, your blood purified, your lungs pumping. It mixes the correct chemicals into whatever food you eat and in the exactly correct proportions needed so you get the benefit of your food.

It does this faster, and more accurately than the greatest chemist on earth could do it for you. If you are injured, whether it be but a pin-prick or a major operation, it sends to the region of your injury whole armies of white blood corpuscles to kill any possible infection and to mend the injury.

O, Man, you are indeed wonderfully made . . . !

This whole sub-conscious process CAN be directed by your conscious mind also. Those who are expert at it can cause the pulse on one side of the body to differ with the pulse on the other side. They can produce that peculiar state of seeming death that is called suspended animation.

But even those who are not expert can conquer disease and ill-health by mental direction. By right thinking in Faith, by the use of Affirmations, by a REAL belief in The Power of Prayer; they can overcome any physical disturbance within their system. There are countless cases of record wherein tumors seemed to dissolve overnight, cataracts vanish, and countless other seeming miracles occur.

"ACCORDING TO YOUR FAITH, **BE IT DONE** UNTO YOU"
said Jesus.
"PICK UP THY BED, AND WALK"

Remember that all physical things are subject unto the Spirit. A bar of iron that seems so solidly real, is made up of countless atoms. The atoms in turn are composed of electrons, nuetrons, protons; infinitely small specks of pure energy—SPIRIT.

There is nothing actually solid about a bar of iron. It only seems solid in our present range of vision, and that is true of everything in this physical world.

Everything, including your body and my body. We are not solid. Our flesh and bones are made up of atoms too, and they in turn are made up of infinitely tiny specks . . . of energy . . . SPIRIT. And the Spirit is of God. The energy is God's and He directs it in Paths that are Perfect.

It is only when His Light is interfered with that inharmonic conditions are set up. These "interference patterns" (as they are called in the science of engineering) produce the disharmony. All that we need to do is to attune our consciousness and our Being to God again to become well.

Cut out the interference. Vibrate in harmony with Him. Direct your attention to Him and His attention to the part of you that is in disharmony. Ask that He re-harmonize you. That He direct His Light into your understanding. Do this in Faith as you talk with Him.

Use an Affirmative statement of Faith as you image the perfection you desire. Continue with the Affirmation until the image of health is Created.

HOW PRAYER CAN BE USED TO PRODUCE DESIRED RESULTS AND WHY IT SOMETIMES SEEMS NOT TO WORK:

So many people are of the opinion that prayer generally does not work. Most people believe that prayer is answered "sometimes." But they seldom stop to think about WHY it works sometimes and not at others.

There is a reason for this just as there is a reason for all things. First of all, let me say that Prayer, true Prayer, ALWAYS works. It sometimes works even before we can utter it. The answer to true Prayer starts to work instantly. True, it sometimes takes some time for FULFILLMENT, but it STARTS the moment that a prayer is said in FAITH.

Much that passes for Prayer is not Prayer at all. It is said thoughtlessly, mechanically. That is not Prayer. It is just talking to yourself. Words falling on empty air. Your attention is not directed on God and He therefore is not listening. Much that passes for Prayer is directed AT some far away, imaginary, vastly old man sitting on a sort of replica of an earthly tinseled throne with little earthly clouds floating all about. The one who prays thus understands not the Nature of God, but creates an idol in his Mind, to which he prays with little Faith.

How could his faith be great and strong and sure, if he thinks of God as something in the shape of an earthly man, a God who is jealous and wrathful? Without Faith a Prayer is dead. And even Faith without works is dead. But an active Faith directed in Prayer is productive of results, instantly, and that is the only way Prayer can be made to work. In this way it ALWAYS WORKS. God is a God of Love. He is Nature. He is Life. His Spirit is Everywhere. It is in the air you breathe. It is in the food you eat. It is in the earth, in the water, in the clouds, in the Heavens, the Planets, and the Skies. He is in and through the Universe. He is in you and in your neighbor, in your friend and in your brother. He is All in All.

Revere Him! He is ALL POWERFUL. He is ALL INTELLI-GENT. HE IS as conscious of YOU as an individual, as YOU are of HIM.

May you continue along this path upon which you are now progressing. May you, too, grow in mind, spirit and soul by gaining the further understanding which may be yours for the seeking. The door is open. We welcome all those who desire to receive further instruction, for by their seeking of wisdom, do they prove their right to The Companionship of The Mayans.